Faces

Art Coloring Pages
Volume III

By
Kathy Carman Henderson

Faces

Dear fellow artist,

In my third coloring book I've switched from designs, many loosely based on nature, to faces. Again, as in the other volumes, I provide two copies of each page so that you can try different color combinations. You can use realistic shades of pink, tan, and brown. Or you can go crazy and color people with green skin and purple hair.

I use colored pencils, but feel free to try crayons, watercolors, markers, or any other medium you desire. If you are using a medium requiring firm pressure, you may want to put a piece of cardboard under your drawing, so the surface of the next design isn't damaged. If you use a wet medium, I suggest you tear the page out before starting work.

Some of the faces have some suggestion of background, some do not. If you are not familiar with this kind of coloring, may I make some suggestions:

1) Try coloring your backgrounds lighter, bluer, or hazier to make the faces stand out.

2) Start with a couple of lighter colors on your faces, but don't be afraid to use dark colors (even blues, greens, and purples) in the shadows of the face.

3) If you want smooth face tones, several mediums, including pastels and pencils, have blenders that will smooth out your strokes. Let the strokes show to make hair look more realistic.

4) If you would like to learn more about drawing faces on your own, you might like to look at my book The Tiger's Whisker which is one in my "Stories to Learn and Draw By" series.

Most of the faces in this book you would probably classify as content, happy, or even worshipful. One of the purposes of my coloring books is to give a relaxing experience, so I chose expressions that I thought would help accomplish that purpose.

God bless you,
Kathy Carman Henderson

Kathy Carman Henderson

Kathy Carman Henderson

Faces

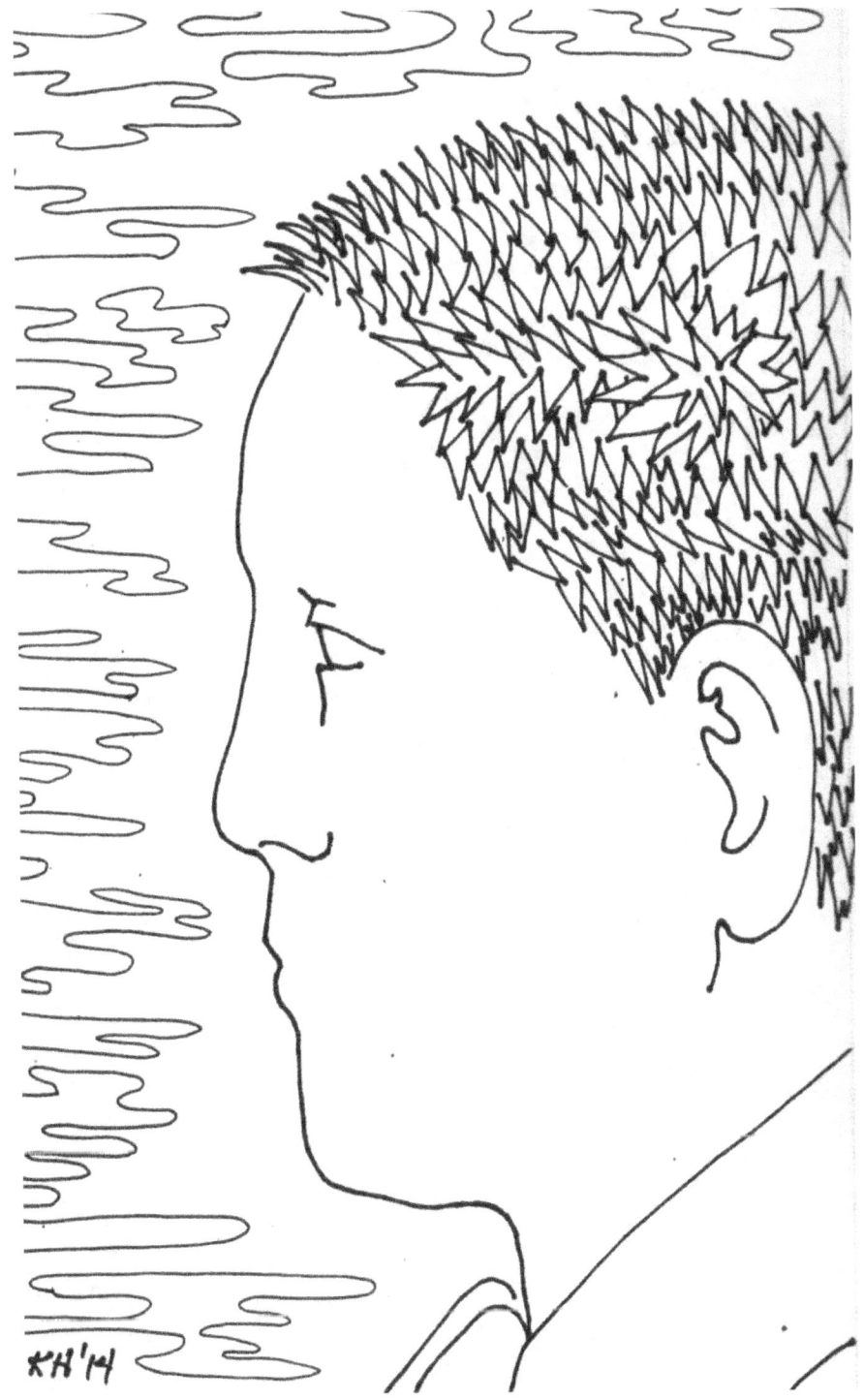

KH'14

Kathy Carman Henderson

Kathy Carman Henderson

Kathy Carman Henderson

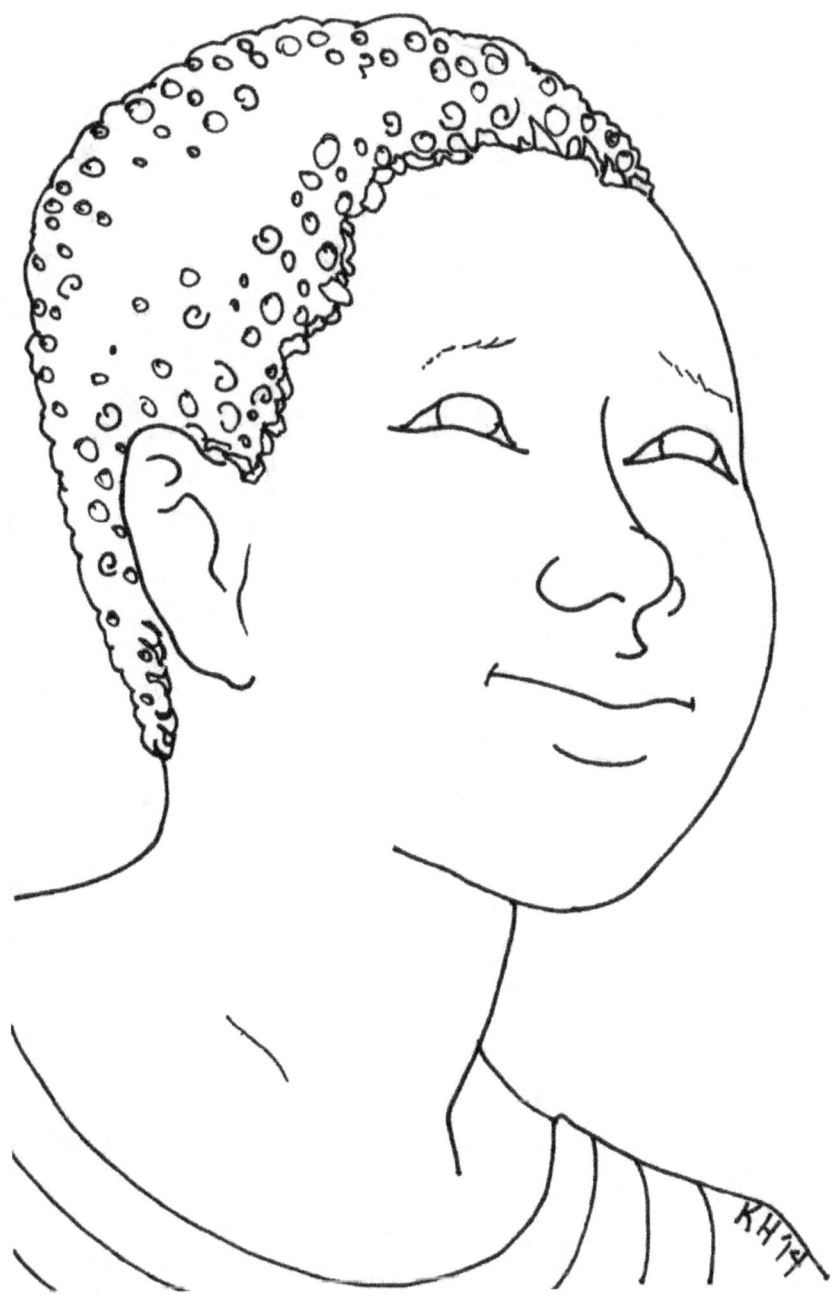

Kathy Carman Henderson

Kathy Carman Henderson

Kathy Carman Henderson

Kathy Carman Henderson

Kathy Carman Henderson

Faces

Kathy Carman Henderson

KH '14

Kathy Carman Henderson

Kathy Carman Henderson

Kathy Carman Henderson

Faces

Kathy Carman Henderson

Kathy Carman Henderson

Faces

Kathy Carman Henderson

Faces

Kathy Carman Henderson

Kathy Carman Henderson

KH'14

Kathy Carman Henderson

Faces

Kathy Carman Henderson

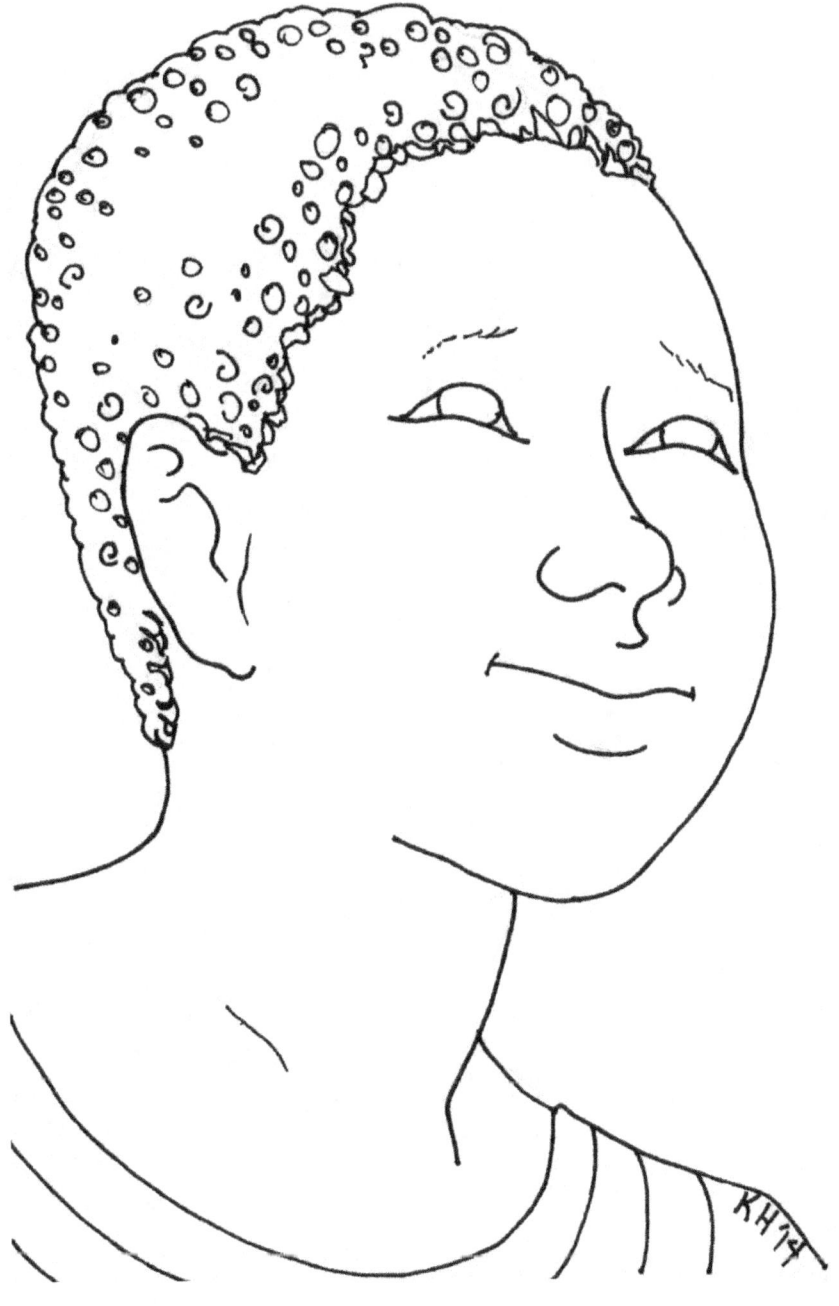

Kathy Carman Henderson

Kathy Carman Henderson

Kathy Carman Henderson

Kathy Carman Henderson

Kathy Carman Henderson

Faces

Kathy Carman Henderson

KH '14

Kathy Carman Henderson

Kathy Carman Henderson

Kathy Carman Henderson

Faces

Kathy Carman Henderson

Kathy Carman Henderson

Faces

Kathy Carman Henderson

Kathy Carman Henderson

Kathy Carman Henderson

Kathy Carman Henderson is an author, illustrator, and teacher. She started drawing as a young child and continues to find it a valuable part of her life.

Other titles from her include:

Art Coloring Books:
Flow & Flair
Flow & Flowers

Stories to Learn and Draw by:
The Walking Vegetables
The One You Don't See Coming
The Tiger's Whisker
The Grasshopper and the Ant

Fiction Travel Adventure:
Costa Rican Adventure with Ben and Gretchen

Western:
Buck

Inspirational:
Party of the Ages

Books illustrated for author Edna Creekmore Carman:
A Day of Rest
Tender Twig